Simone's Travels

by Allen Young
illustrated by Nicole Wong

PEARSON

Scott
Foresman

Editorial Offices: Glenview, Illinois • Parsippany, New Jersey • New York, New York
Sales Offices: Needham, Massachusetts • Duluth, Georgia • Glenview, Illinois
Coppell, Texas • Ontario, California • Mesa, Arizona

The winter holidays were not turning out the way Simone had hoped. Simone was stuck at home. She had been stuck at home for a week. Outside the wind was blowing and the rain was beating down.

Lindy, Simone's best friend, had gone away to Florida to visit her grandparents. Matt, her classmate who lived across the street, had gone to Arizona to visit his dad.

Simone was bored.

"I don't know what do to!" she told her mom.

"Practice your clarinet!" her mom replied. Simone picked up her clarinet. Misty, the cat, took one look at Simone and bolted out of the room. Simone sounded awful. She just could not get her fingers to move fast enough.

"I can't play!" Simone frowned.

"Read a book," her mom suggested. Simone picked up a book about monkeys and looked at the pictures.

"Mom, where could we go to see monkeys?" she asked.

"Maybe a rain forest," her mom replied.

"Or Africa," Simone said, looking at a map in the book.

"Or Asia," said her mom.

"We could see them in the zoo!" Simone looked at her mom hopefully.

"We can't go to the zoo, Simone. It's raining." Simone slumped into a chair by the window. "I wish we could go *somewhere!*" Simone said.

"Why don't you get out your colored pencils and paper and draw?" her mom asked. Simone's face lit up. Drawing was one of her favorite things to do.

"Maybe I could draw pictures of all the different places I'd like to go!" she grinned.

"That sounds like a good idea," her mom smiled. "I'll make you some hot chocolate."

Simone spread out her supplies. Misty curled up at her feet.

Simone smiled and thought of being on the road to Grandma's farm in Wisconsin. She loved her grandma very much. Any time she visited, it was sure to be fun.

Simone imagined looking out the car window at all the landmarks they passed on the way to Grandma's farm. She would watch the green fields dotted with cows and look for the tall red water tower. She always knew they were close when they passed Carlson's Pond.

Simone loved to sit with Grandma and listen to her stories. Grandma talked about life at the farm before Simone's mom and Uncle Bruce were born.

Simone liked to play games with Grandma and the farmhands who plowed the fields. Simone enjoyed riding with them on the tractor, with the fresh air blowing in her face.

Simone made up names for all the animals. She had named the rooster "Mr. Dean" because he looked just like Mr. Dean, her music teacher. She had named one of the horses "Tuftytoes" because his feet were covered with fluffy hair.

Simone picked up her pencil and began drawing a picture of Grandma's farm. As she drew, Simone thought about what it would be like to live in Wisconsin with Grandma. She knew she would have to get up very early every day to feed the chickens.

Simone knew that if she lived on the farm, she would always be busy. Even though living in Wisconsin seemed like it would be fun, Simone knew that it would take a while to adjust to life on the farm. She would miss life in her town if she left.

Simone loved her town, especially in the summer and the fall.

Simone's hometown, Seahaven, was known for its apple groves. There were miles and miles of trees. Simone's dad said they grew the best apples in the world.

Simone and her father spent many early fall weekends walking through the groves and picking apples. Then she would help her mom bake apple pies. She always took an extra pie over to her friend Lindy who lived next door.

Simone loved the apple groves but her favorite part of living in Seahaven wasn't the apples.

What made Seahaven home for Simone were all the things she did and all the people she knew. Simone loved going to Mrs. Stein's Dance Studio, where she took ballet classes. Last summer Simone and Lindy had performed in a big dance recital. Everyone in town came to watch!

Sometimes Simone, Lindy, and their moms would go to the Centurion, the town's movie theatre. Next to the Centurion was the girls' favorite ice cream parlor.

Simone could not imagine living any place better than Seahaven.

Simone looked out the window. It wouldn't be summer or fall again for a long while. Simone sighed.

"Mom, what else can I draw?" she asked.

"What about your trip to New York City?" her mom suggested.

Simone thought about how that summer she had traveled with Lindy and her mom to New York City.

Everything they had seen in New York City was unexpected. It was the biggest, loudest, fastest, and most colorful place Simone could imagine.

Simone, Lindy, and her mom took a walking tour of Manhattan. They walked very far, but there was so much to see Simone hardly noticed the many miles they covered.

Simone's favorite part was looking for gargoyles on the buildings. She liked best the gargoyles that were carved to look like strange, scary animals. Simone and Lindy made up stories about each of the gargoyles they saw.

In Seahaven, Simone was used to walking or driving to the store, but in New York City, they took the subway. Simone and Lindy tried to follow the subway map so they could tell where their train would stop next.

Once they took a ride in a taxi. Simone was amazed by how many other cars and people there were on the road.

If New York City was loud, fast, and big, Lake Wellington was quiet, slow, and small. Lake Wellington was a lakeside town where Simone sometimes visited her dad's sister, Aunt Betsy. She decided to draw Lake Wellington next.

Lake Wellington was smaller than Seahaven, with only a small general store, a restaurant, a store that rented movies, and a bakery. The people who lived in Lake Wellington were friendly.

Simone loved the smell of fresh bread outside the bakery. When Simone and Aunt Betsy went to buy bread, Miss Rose, the bakery manager, always gave Simone a small, freshly-baked treat.

Simone's dad loved Lake Wellington because it was his favorite place to go fishing.

Sometimes Simone would go fishing with Dad. She loved to chat with him in the canoe. Sometimes Simone and her friends would play together on the dock. When it got too hot they would go swimming in the clear water. In the winter, the lake sometimes froze over, so Simone, her mother, and Aunt Betsy would go skating.

The memories of her trips had made Simone feel better. She put all her pictures in order and called to her mom.

"Mom! Come see my pictures!"

"Wow!" said Simone's mom. "You've been busy!"

"Which one do you like best?" Simone asked.

Simone's mom listened as Simone talked about the places and people she had drawn.

Simone and her mom laughed at the picture of Grandma's rooster.

"He *does* look like Mr. Dean!" her mom smiled.

"I like my New York City gargoyle picture," said Simone, holding it up proudly.

"I do too," said her mom. "But I think my favorite picture is this one." Simone's mom held up a picture of Simone, her dad, and Aunt Betsy fishing from a canoe in Lake Wellington.

Simone looked out the window. It had stopped raining and the Sun was shining through the bare tree branches. Simone had an idea.

"Mom! Can we visit Aunt Betsy this week? I could give her my picture as a gift!"

"I think she would love that," said Simone's mom. "Now clean up and you can help me bake some banana bread!"

Learning About Different Places

Living in a big city, such as New York City, can be very different from living in a small town, such as Lake Wellington. Living in a place like Seahaven is very different from living on a farm in Wisconsin. Imagine how different it might be to live in another country!

It is always good to see and learn about other places in the world. When you meet someone from another place, you can find out things you never knew before. Next time you take a trip or meet someone from another place, ask a lot of questions. You never know what you might learn!